Grocery Store

By Jennifer Colby

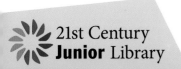
21st Century
Junior Library

Published in the United States of America by
Cherry Lake Publishing
Ann Arbor, Michigan
www.cherrylakepublishing.com

Content Adviser: Becky Cairati, Former Grocery Store Crew Member
Reading Adviser: Marla Conn MS, Ed., Literacy specialist, Read-Ability, Inc.

Photo Credits: © Monkey Business Images/Shutterstock Images, cover, 1, 4, 18, 20; © Robert Kneschke/
Shutterstock Images, 6; ©Tyler Olson/Shutterstock Images, 8; ©XiXinXing/iStock Images, 10;
© wavebreakmedia/Shutterstock Images, 12; © andresr/iStock Images, 14;
© Minerva Studio/Shutterstock Images, 16

Library of Congress Cataloging-in-Publication Data
Names: Colby, Jennifer, 1971- author.
Title: Grocery store / by Jennifer Colby.
Description: Ann Arbor : Cherry Lake Publishing, [2016] | Series: 21st
   century junior library | Series: Explore a workplace | Includes
   bibliographical references and index.
Identifiers: LCCN 2015047471| ISBN 9781634710732 (hardcover) | ISBN 9781634711722 (pdf) |
ISBN 9781634712712 (pbk.) | ISBN 9781634713702 (ebook)
Subjects: LCSH: Supermarkets—Juvenile literature. | Grocery trade—Juvenile
   literature.
Classification: LCC HF5469 .C59 2016 | DDC 381/.456413—dc23
LC record available at http://lccn.loc.gov/2015047471

Cherry Lake Publishing would like to acknowledge the work of The Partnership for 21st Century Learning.
Please visit *www.p21.org* for more information.

Printed in the United States of America
Corporate Graphics

CONTENTS

You can buy many things at a grocery store.

What Is a Grocery Store?

You are in a store with **aisles**. The aisles have shelves of food. Where are you? You are at a grocery store. Your shopping cart has groceries in it. You are ready to pay. A **cashier** invites you to the **cash register**. The cashier is a worker who helps your family at the grocery store.

There are many different jobs to do at a grocery store.

People buy food at a grocery store. They also buy other items. Do you go shopping with your parents? What do you buy? Many people do lots of different jobs in grocery stores. They all work together. They help you find the things that you need. Let's look at some grocery store workers.

Make a Guess!

Guess how many cash registers are at your grocery store. Write down your guess. Count them the next time you go there. Was your guess right?

One section of the grocery store has produce.

Grocery Store Workers

Have you seen different sections in a grocery store? One section has fruits and vegetables. This is the **produce** section. Another has breads and cakes. This is the bakery section. Each section has workers to help you.

A worker must place food items on shelves.

The **deli** person slices meat and cheese for you. You talk to a baker when you order a cake. A produce worker shows you where your favorite fruit is.

Who else works in the store? **Stock clerks** place food and other items on shelves. Cashiers add up your shopping cart. They take your money and put it in the cash register. A **bagger** puts the things you bought in bags to take home.

A manager is in charge of each section of the store.

Who is in charge of the workers? There is a **manager** to take care of each section of the store. Managers **train** the workers in their section. They also order things. Managers make sure their sections have items that are fresh and ready for customers to buy.

Think!

Look around the store the next time you go grocery shopping. Try to spot workers in each section of the store. How many sections does it have? Which section do you like?

Store managers talk to people.

The store manager is in charge of the whole grocery store. The store manager hires the workers. Thinking of new ways to sell things is the store manager's job. The store manager wants the grocery store to be a nice place to shop. It is important that customers are happy and come back!

It takes many workers to run a grocery store. Each worker plays an important part in bringing food to your family!

Some grocery store workers wear aprons.
This helps you know who works in the store.

Do You Want to Work at a Grocery Store?

Would you like to work in a grocery store? You can start learning now! Talk to workers when you go shopping. Find out what they like about their jobs. What do you like about the store?

A list helps you while you shop.

Grocery store workers need to be **organized**. They must know where items are. They must know what things cost. They must keep track of when to restock items.

Are you organized? Ask your parents if you can write the next grocery list. Check your pantry. Check your refrigerator. What do you need? Write it down. Check off the items on your list when you go shopping.

It is important for grocery store workers to be friendly and polite to customers.

A grocery store is a fun place to work. Each worker has a job to do. We all need to shop for groceries. Do you like to go to the store? You can work at a grocery store someday!

Create!

Turn your kitchen into a store. Ask a parent for help. Make a produce section. Make a bakery section. Give each item a price. Set up an area with a calculator and bags. Ask your family to shop in your store.

GLOSSARY

aisles (AYLZ) passages between shelves in a store where customers walk

bagger (BAG-ur) a worker who puts groceries in bags for customers

cashier (kah-SHEER) a worker who adds up what shoppers owe and accepts their payment

cash register (KASH REJ-i-stur) a machine that cashiers use to store money and add up shoppers' bills

deli (DEL-ee) a place where you can buy foods that are already cooked or prepared, such as meats, cheese, salads, and sandwiches

manager (MAN-uh-jur) a person who is in charge

organized (OR-guh-nyzd) having things arranged or planned in a particular way

produce (PROH-duse) fresh fruits and vegetables

stock clerks (STAHK KLURKS) workers who put items on store shelves

train (TRAYN) to teach someone a skill

FIND OUT MORE

BOOKS

Balconi, Michelle, and Arthur Laffer. *Let's Chat About Economics! Basic Principles Through Everyday Scenarios*. Grosse Pointe Woods, MI : Gichigami Press, 2014.

Castaldo, Nancy. *The Story of Seeds: From Mendel's Garden to Your Plate, and How There's More of Less to Eat Around the World*. Boston: HMH Books for Young Readers, 2016.

WEB SITES

KidsHealth—Healthy Food Shopping
http://kidshealth.org/parent/nutrition_center/healthy_eating/food_shopping.html
Learn how to make healthy choices at the grocery store.

PBS Kids—Arthur: Supermarket Adventure
http://pbskids.org/arthur/games/supermarket/supermarket.html
Learn about different types of food at the grocery store as you help D.W. shop in this online game.

INDEX

ABOUT THE AUTHOR

Jennifer Colby is the author of many books for children. When she was a kid, she wanted to be a bagger at the grocery store. Now she is a high school librarian in Michigan. She still enjoys bagging her own groceries.